Russian Alphabet / Русский Алфавит

	А Page 8 - 9	Б Page 10 - 11	В Page 12 - 13	
Г Page 14 - 15	Д Page 16 - 17	Е Page 18 - 19	Ё Page 20 - 21	Ж Page 22 - 23
З Page 24 - 25	И Page 26 - 27	Й Page 28 - 29	К Page 30 - 31	Л Page 32 - 33
М Page 34 - 35	Н Page 36 - 37	О Page 38 - 39	П Page 40-41	Р Page 42 - 43
С Page 44 - 45	Т Page 46 - 47	У Page 48 - 49	Ф Page 50 - 51	Х Page 52 - 53
Ц Page 54 - 55	Ч Page 56 - 57	Ш Page 58 - 59	Щ Page 60 - 61	Ъ Page 62 - 63
Ы Page 64 - 65	Ь Page 66 - 67	Э Page 68 - 69	Ю Page 70 - 71	Я Page 72 - 73

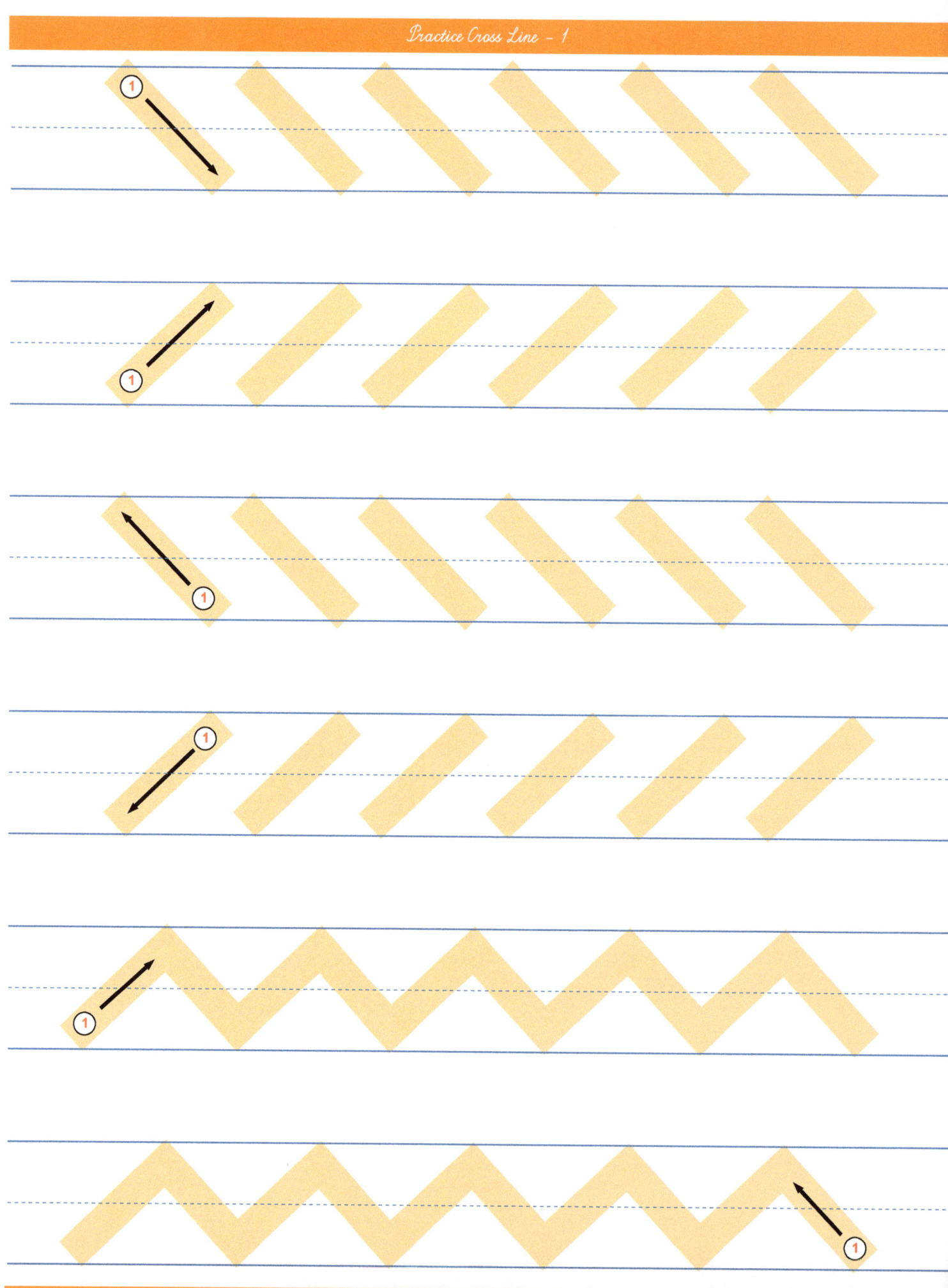

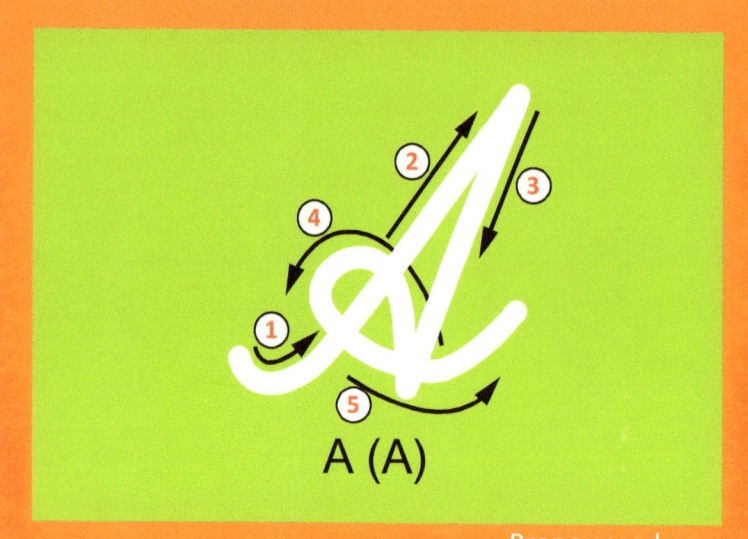

A (A)

Апельсин / Apel'seen / Orange

Pronounced as sound of "a" in "Star"

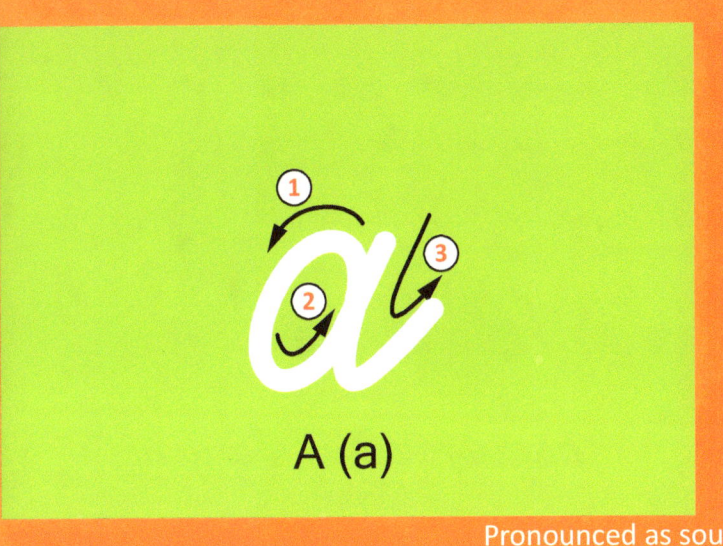

A (a)

Pronounced as sound of "a" in "Ask"

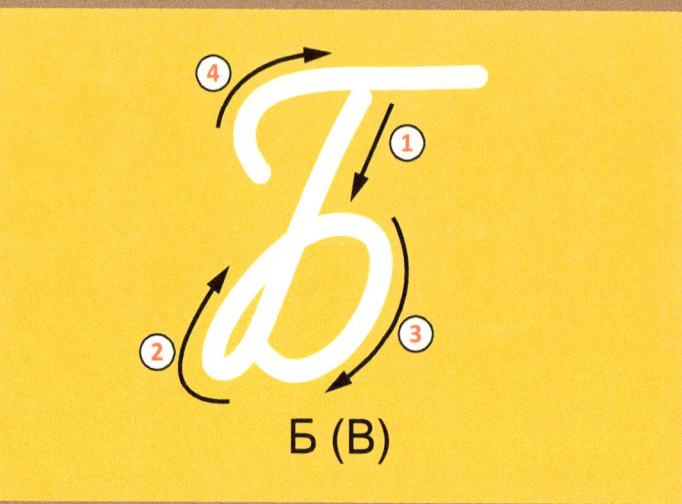

Б (B)

Белка/Belka/Squirrel

Pronounced as sound of "b" in "Banana"

Б (Б)

Pronounced as sound of "b" in "Bear"

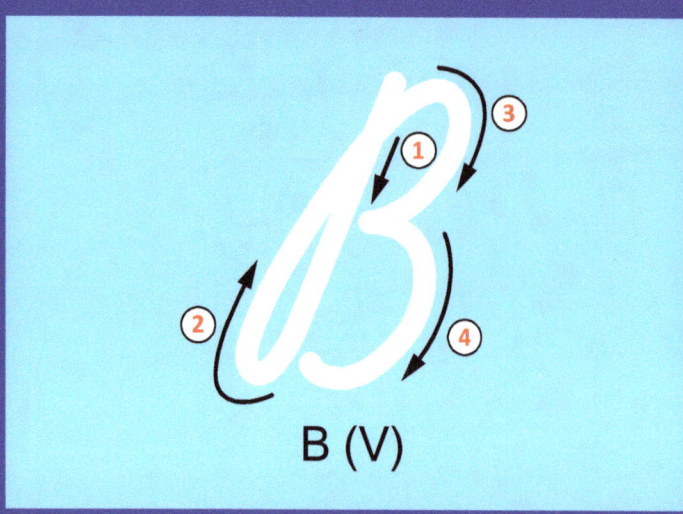

В (V)

Велосипед/Veloseeped/Bicycle

Pronounced as sound of "v" in "Visit"

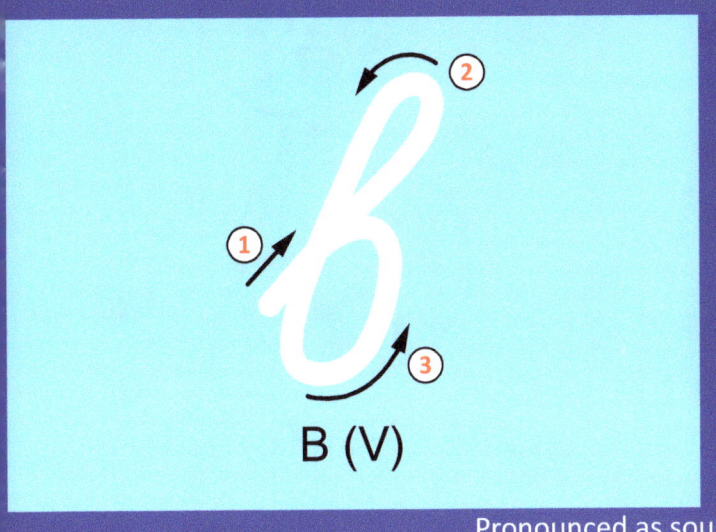

B (V)

Pronounced as sound of "v" in "Voice"

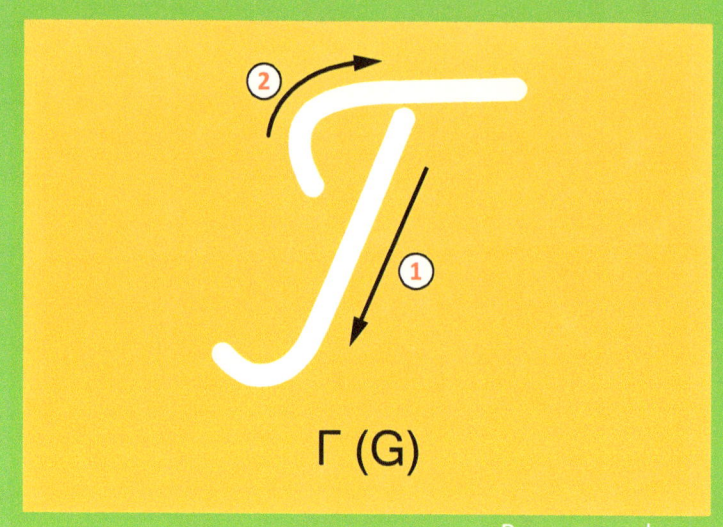

Г (G)

Груша/Groosha/Pear

Pronounced as sound of "g" in "Get"

Pronounced as sound of "g" in "Guard"

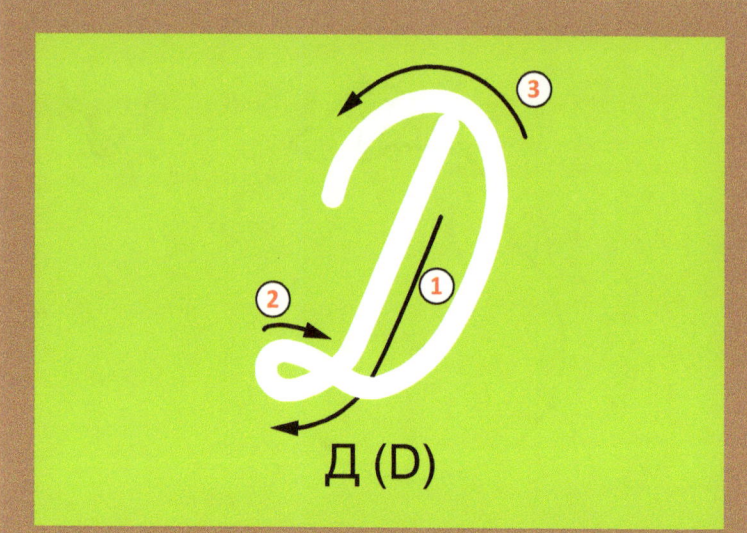

Д (D)

Дерево/Derevo/Tree

Pronounced as sound of "d" in "Dolphin"

Д (D)

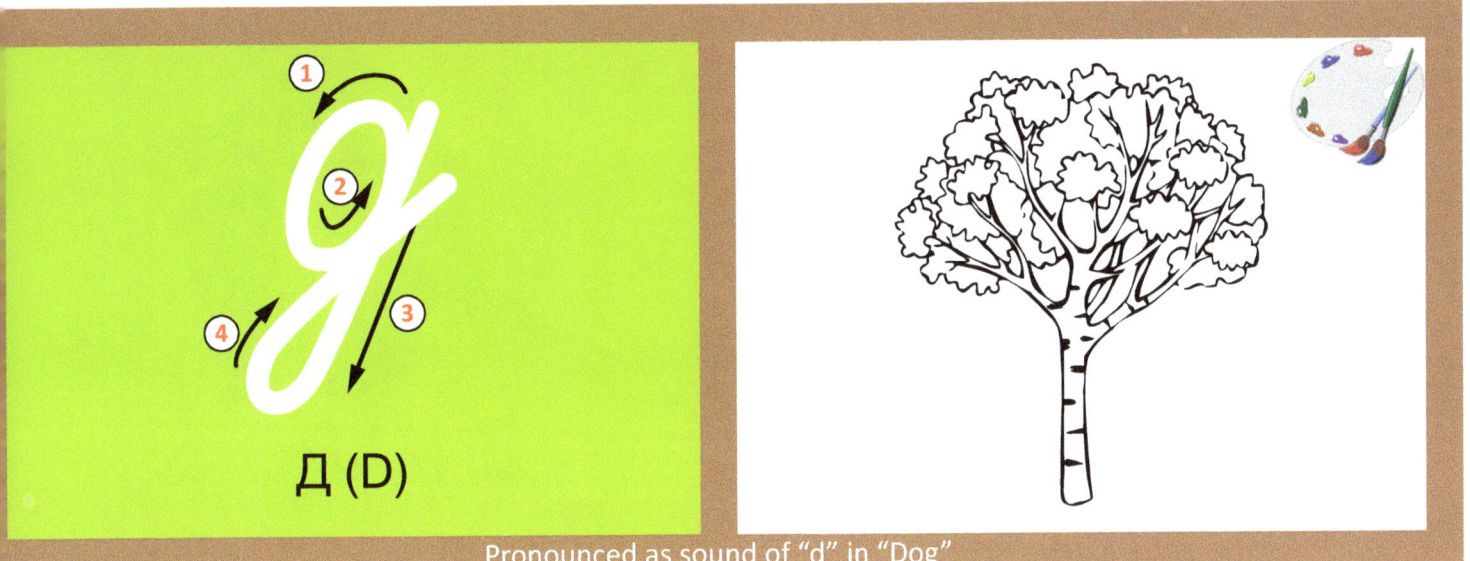

Pronounced as sound of “d” in “Dog”

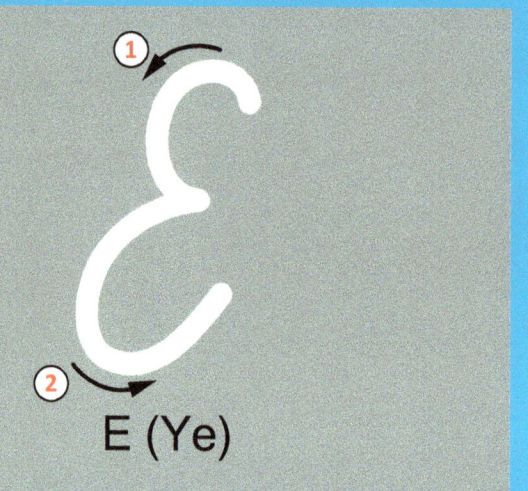

E (Ye)

Енот/Yenot/Raccoon

Pronounced as sound of "ye" in "Yet"

Pronounced as sound of "ye" in "Yes"

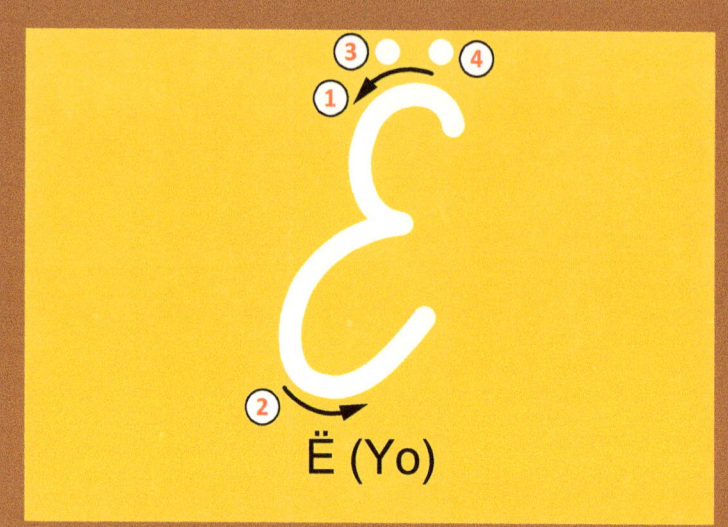

Ё (Yo)

Ёж / Yozh / Hedgehog

Pronounced as sound of "yo" in "Yo yo"

Ë (Yo)

Pronounced as sound of "yo" in "Yonder"

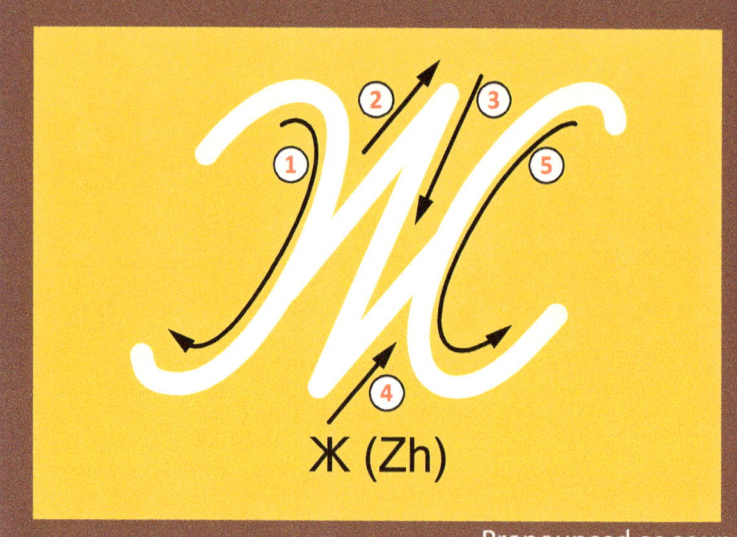
Ж (Zh)

Жираф/Zheeraf/Giraffe

Pronounced as sound of "s" in "Measure"

Ж (Zh)

Pronounced as sound of "g" in "Beige"

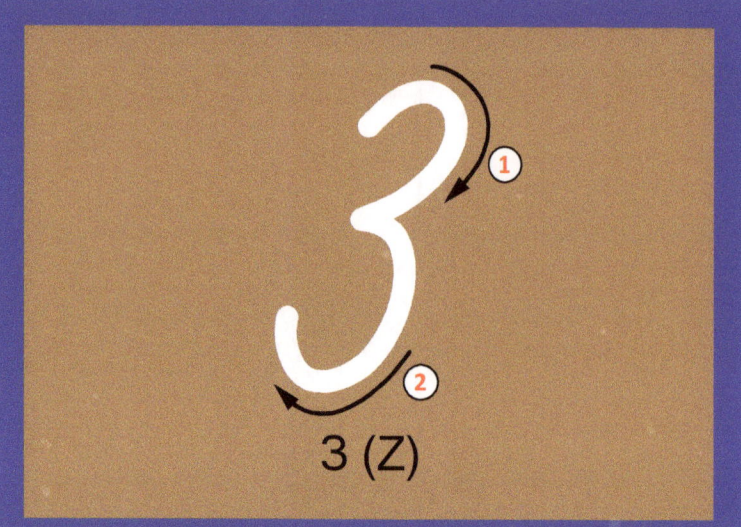

З (Z)

Зебра/Zebra/Zebra

Pronounced as sound of "z" in "Zero"

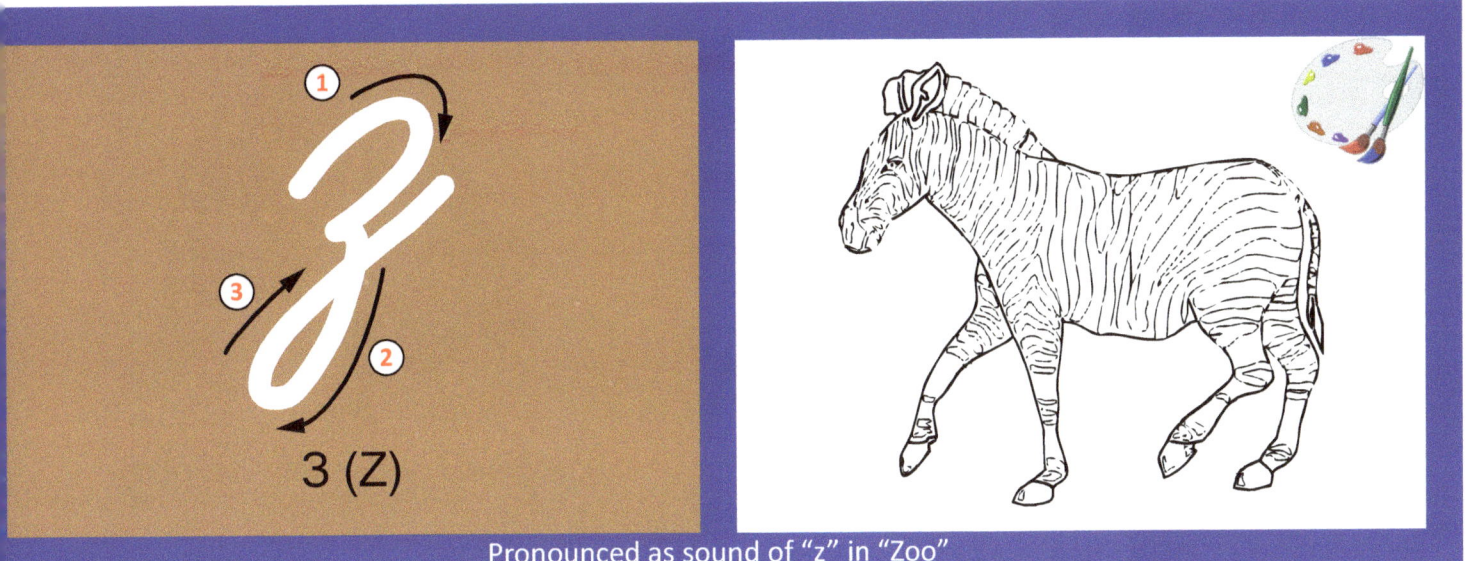

Pronounced as sound of "z" in "Zoo"

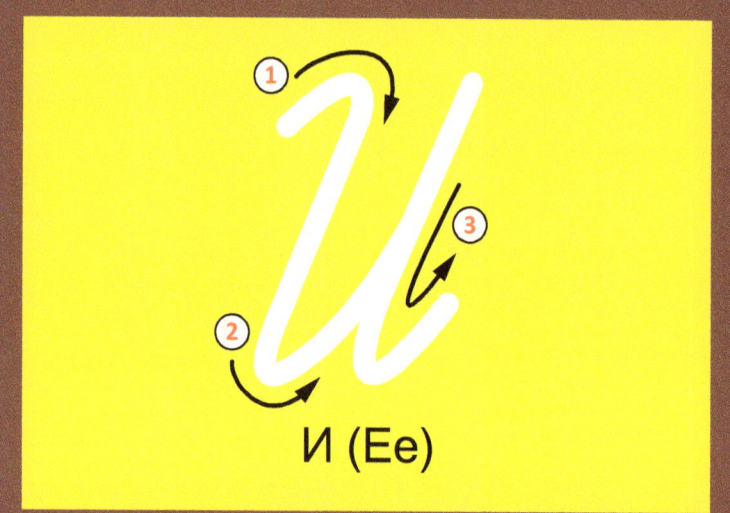

И (Ее)

Индюк / Eendyuk / Turkey

Pronounced as sound of "ee" in "Eel"

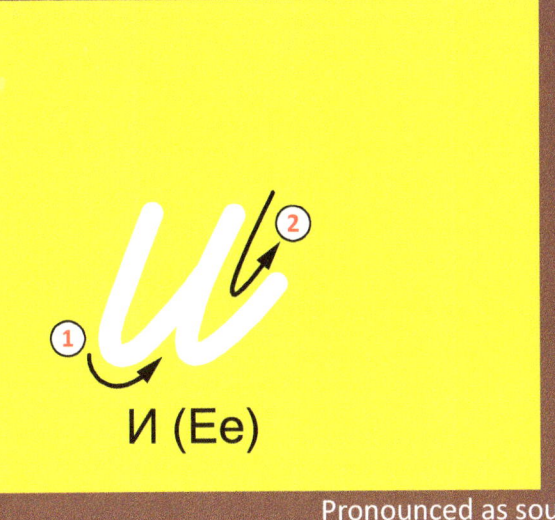

И (Ee)

Pronounced as sound of "ee" in "See"

Й (Y)

Йогурт / Yogurt / Yogurt

Pronounced as sound of "y" in "Yogurt"

Pronounced as sound of "y" in "Toy"

K (K)

Kom/Kot/Cat

Pronounced as sound of "k" in "Kitten"

K (K)

Pronounced as sound of "c" in "Cat"

Л (L)

Лиса/Leesa/Fox

Pronounced as sound of "l" in "Leg"

Pronounced as sound of "l" in "Lost"

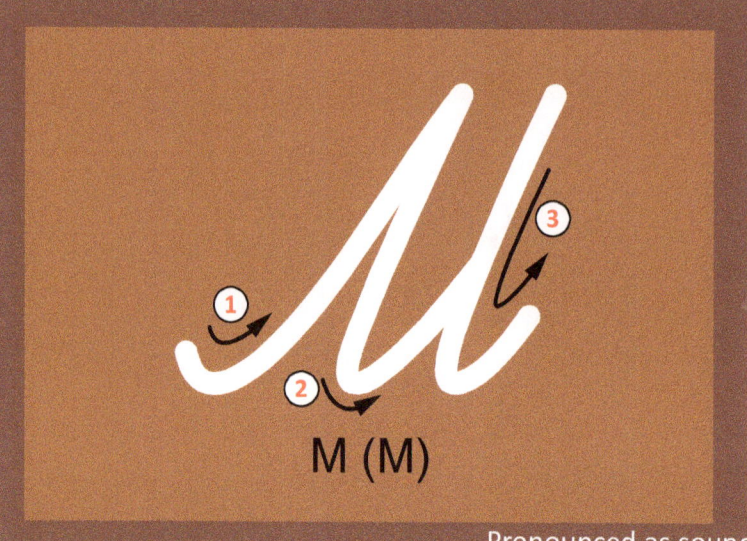

M (M)

Pronounced as sound of "m" in "More"

Мяч/Myach/Ball

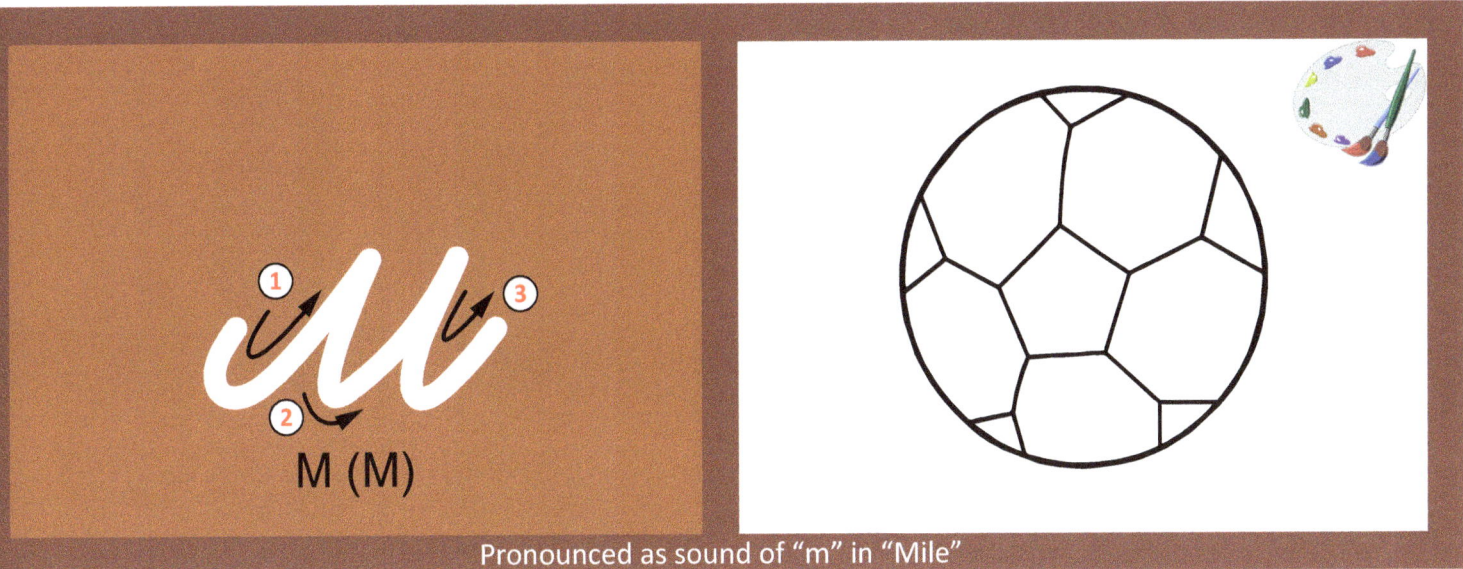

Pronounced as sound of "m" in "Mile"

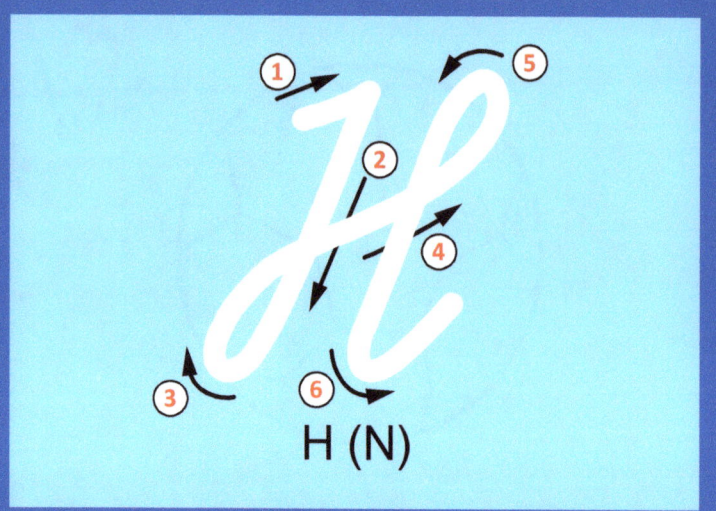
H (N)

Носки / Noski / Socks

Pronounced as sound of "n" in "Next"

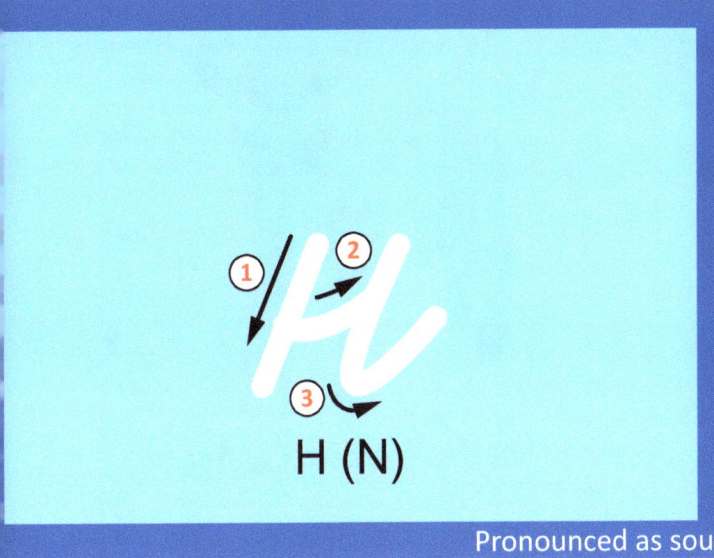

H (N)

Pronounced as sound of "n" in "Nord"

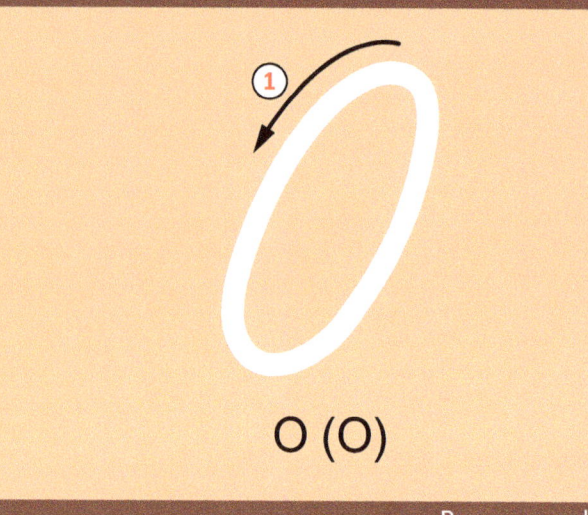

O (O)

Obya / Ovtsa / Sheep

Pronounced as sound of "o" in "Orange"

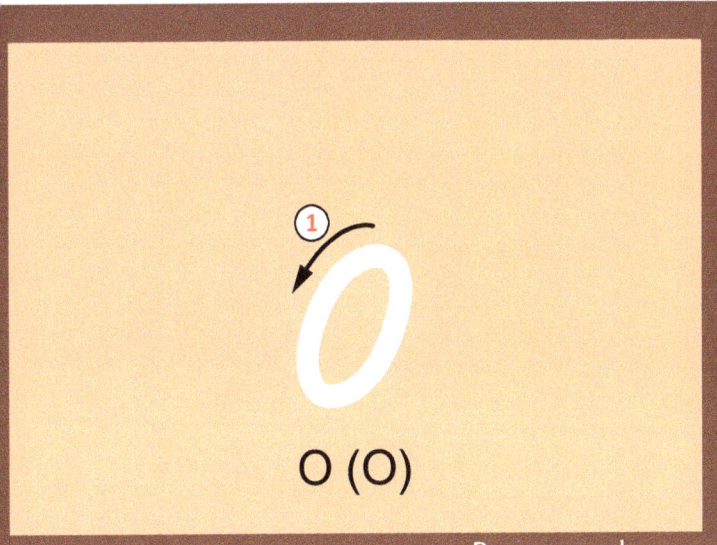

O (O)

Pronounced as sound of "o" in "Ocean"

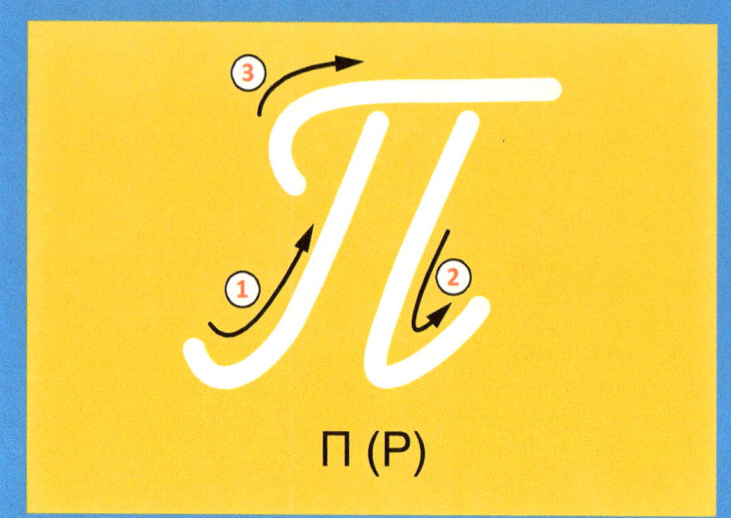

П (P)

Поезд/Poezd/Train

Pronounced as sound of "p" in "Penguin"

П (Р)

Pronounced as sound of "p" in "Parrot"

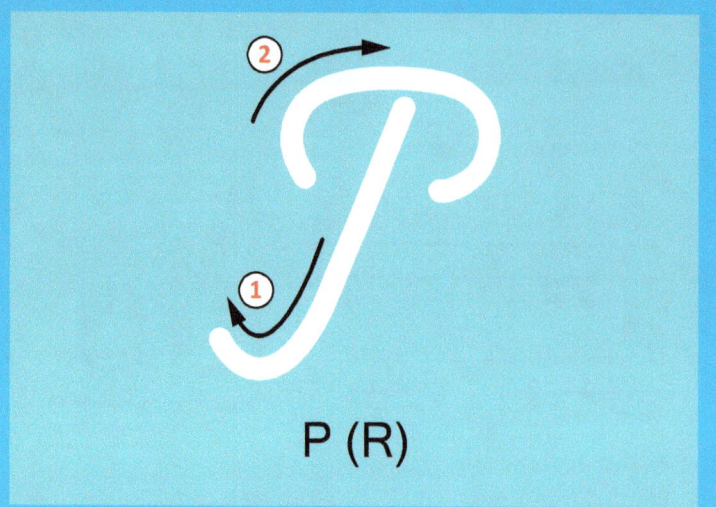

P (R)

Рыба/Riba/Fish

Pronounced as sound of "r" in "Red"

P (R)

Pronounced as sound of "r" in "River"

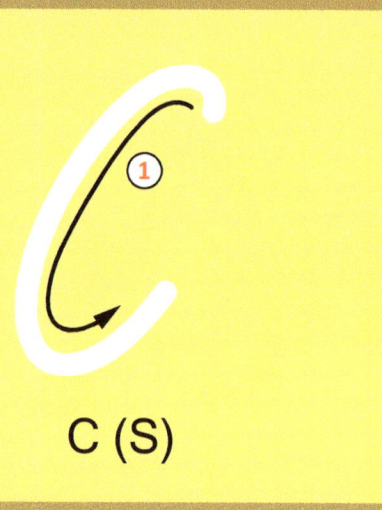

С (S)

Собака / Sobaka / Dog

Pronounced as sound of "s" in "Storm"

C (S)

Pronounced as sound of "s" in "Saint"

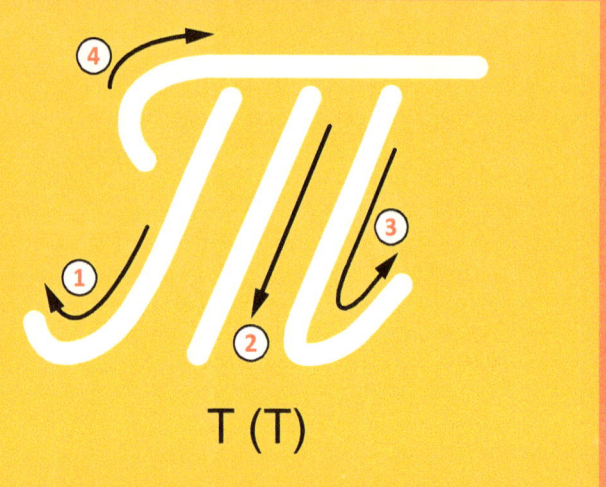

Т (T)

Торт/Tort/Cake

Pronounced as sound of "t" in "Tiger"

T (T)

Pronounced as sound of "t" in "Terra"

m m m m m m m m m
m m m m m m m m
m m m m m m m
m m m m m m
m m m m m
m m m m
m m m
m m
m

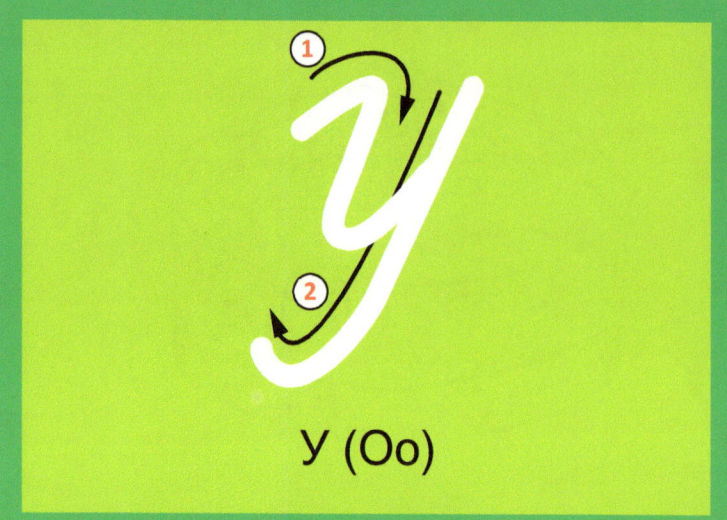

у (Oo)

Утка/Ootka/Duck

Pronounced as sound of "oo" in "Toon"

У (Oo)

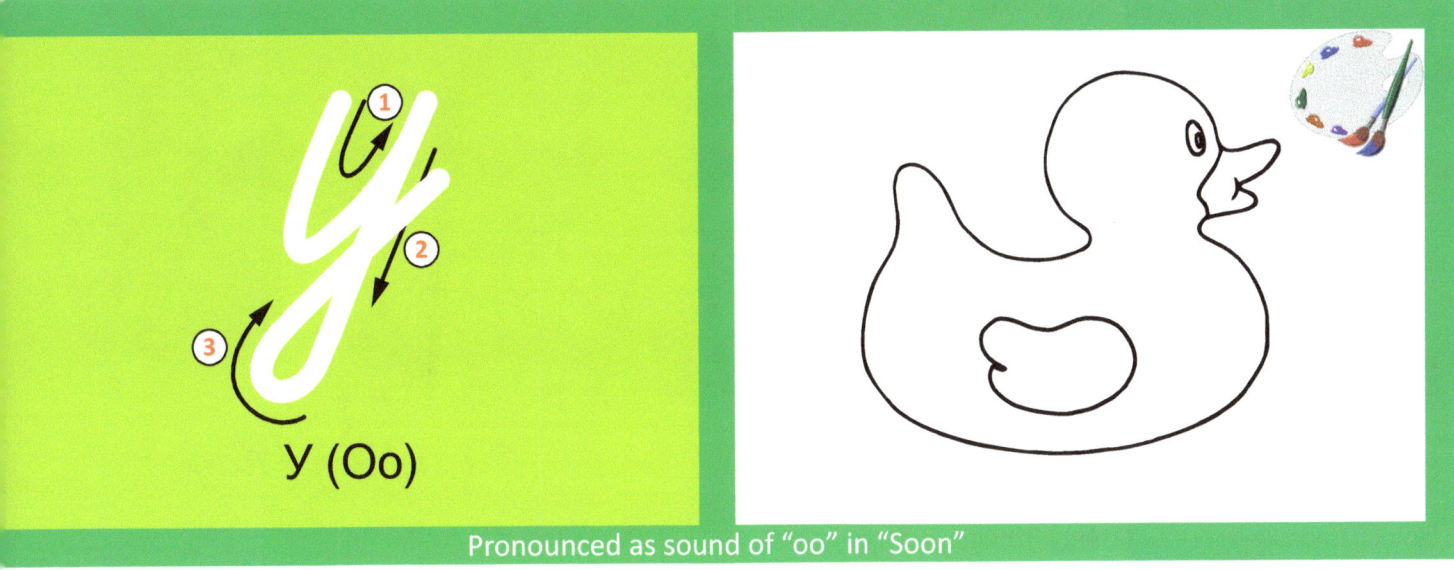

Pronounced as sound of “oo” in “Soon”

Ф (F)

Флаг/Flag/Flag

Pronounced as sound of "f" in "Flamingo"

Φ (F)

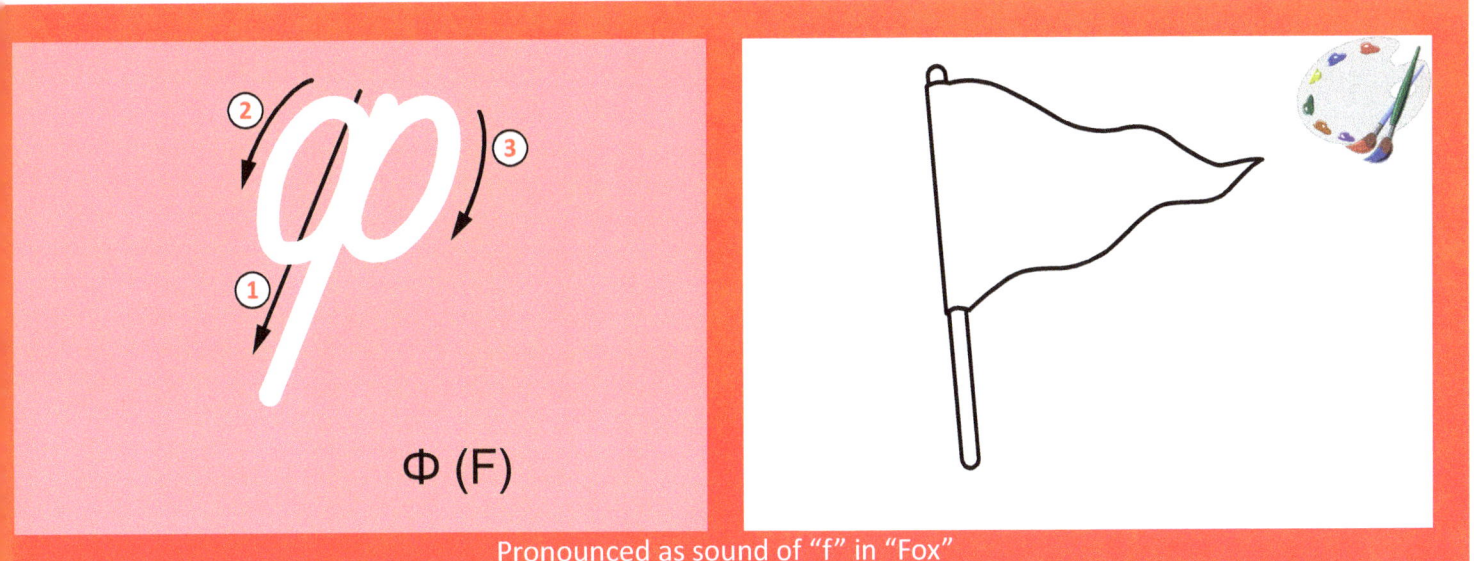

Pronounced as sound of "f" in "Fox"

X (Х)

Хлеб/Hleb/Bread

Pronounced as sound of "h" in "Hello"

X (H)

Pronounced as sound of "h" in "Happy"

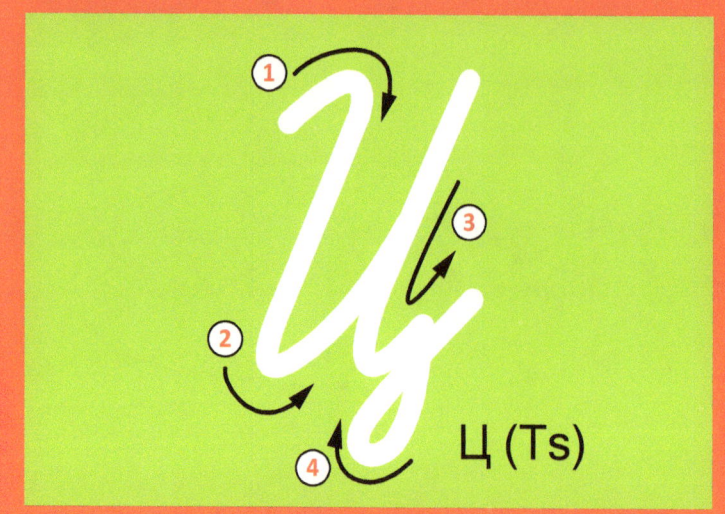

Ц (Ts)

Цветок/Tsvetok/Flower

Pronounced as sound of "ts" in "Darts"

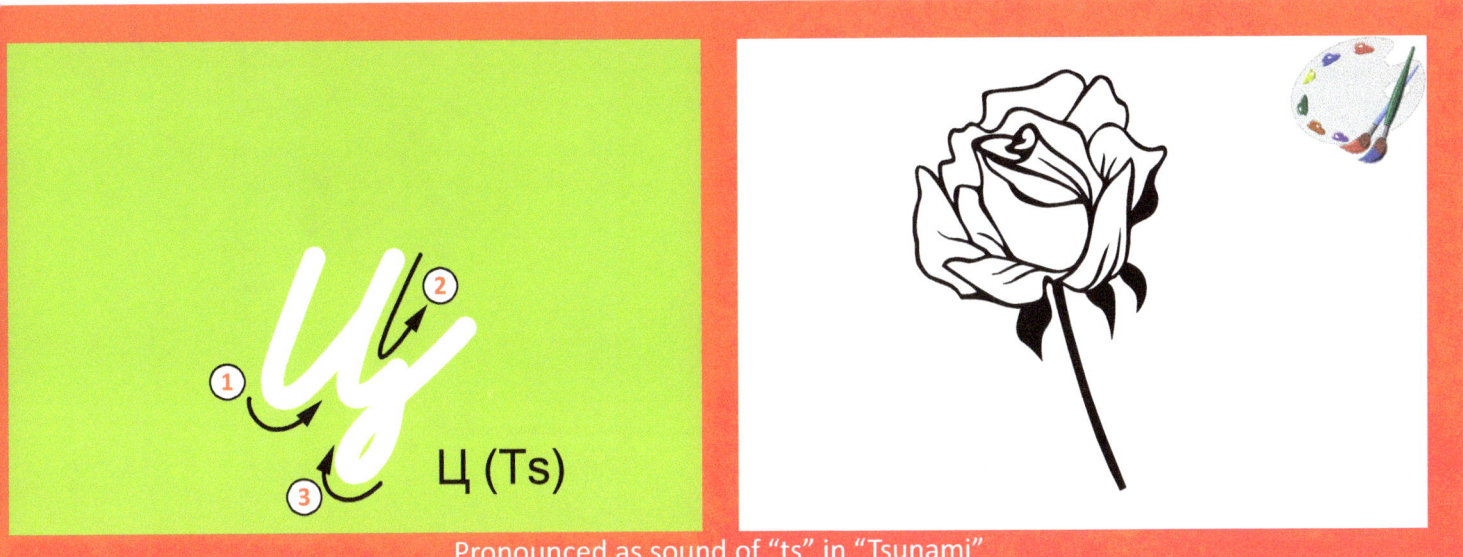

Ц (Ts)

Pronounced as sound of "ts" in "Tsunami"

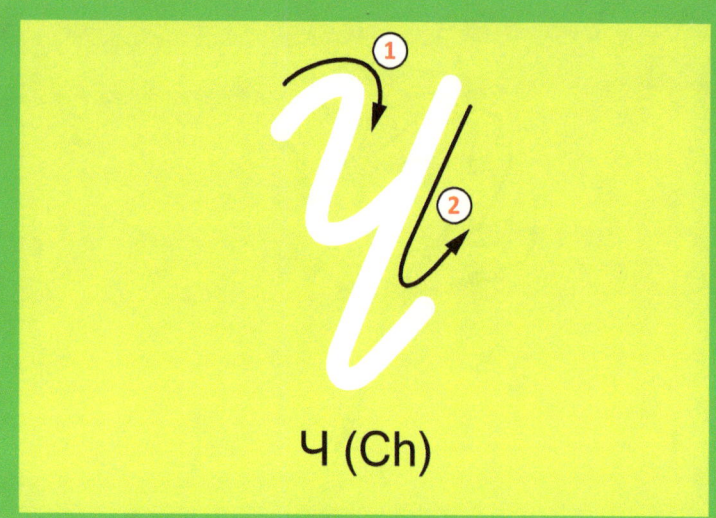

Ч (Ch)

Черепаха/Cherepaha/Turtle

Pronounced as sound of "ch" in "Sandwich"

Ч (Ch)

Pronounced as sound of "ch" in "Change"

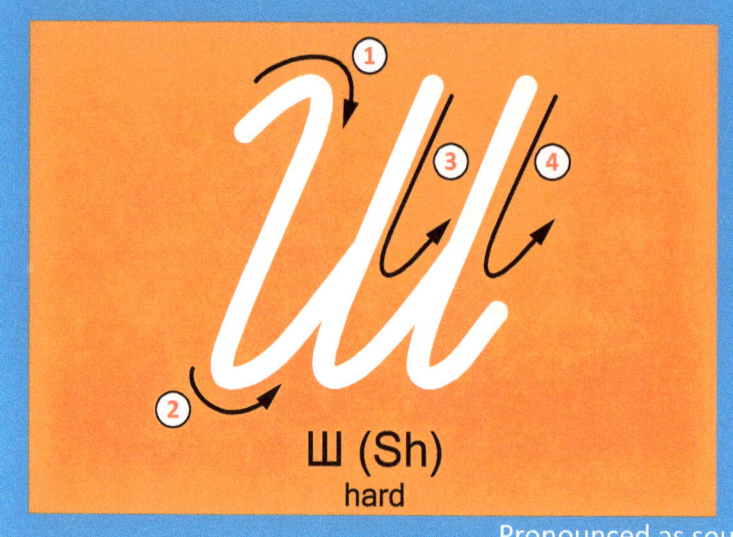

Ш (Sh)
hard

Шар/Shar/Baloon

Pronounced as sound of "sh" in "She"

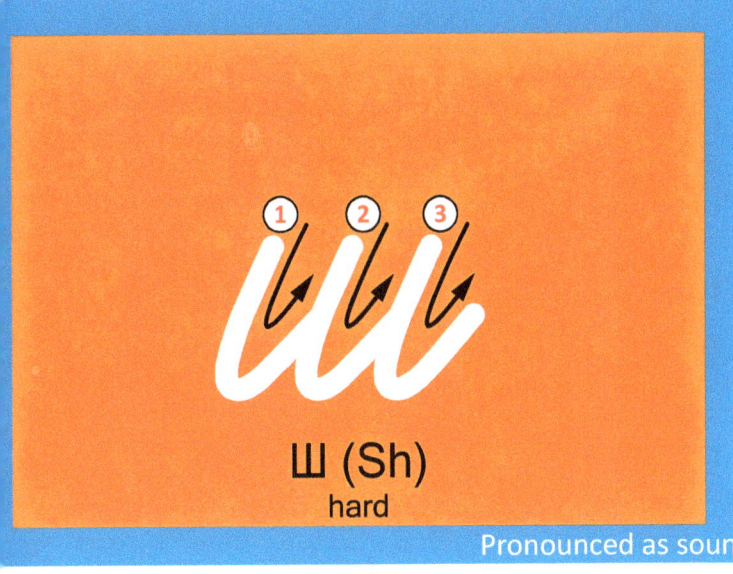

Ш (Sh)
hard

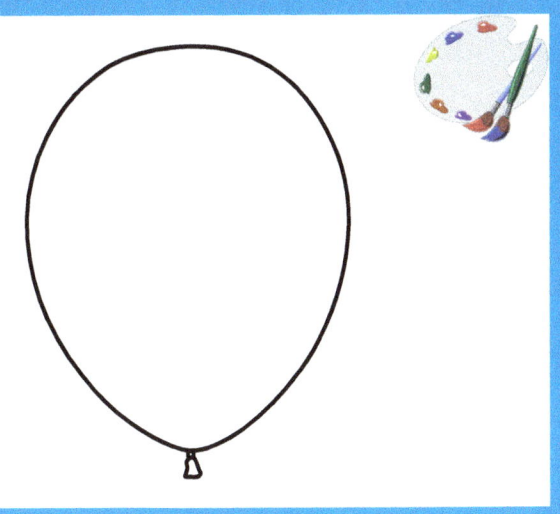

Pronounced as sound of "sh" in "Dish"

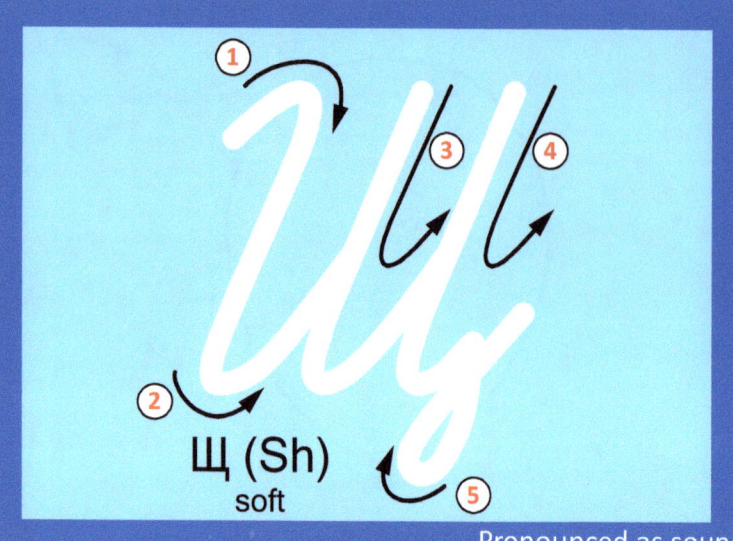

Щ (Sh) soft

Pronounced as sound of "sh" in "Sheep"

Щётка / Shchyotka / Brush

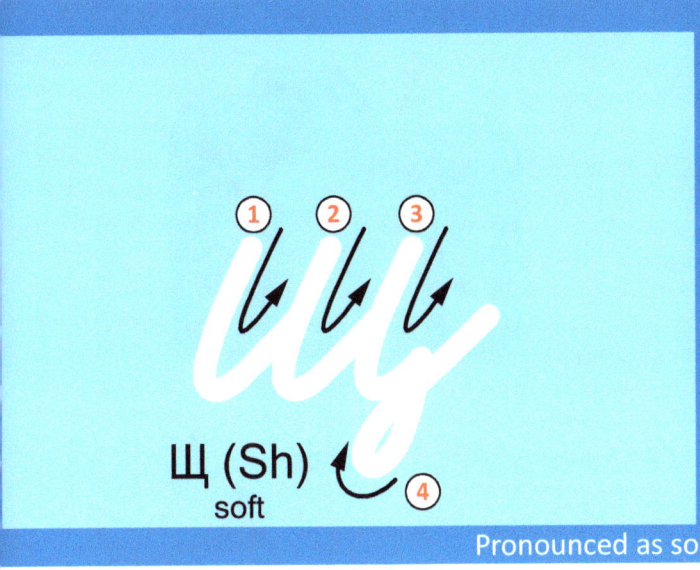

Щ (Sh) soft

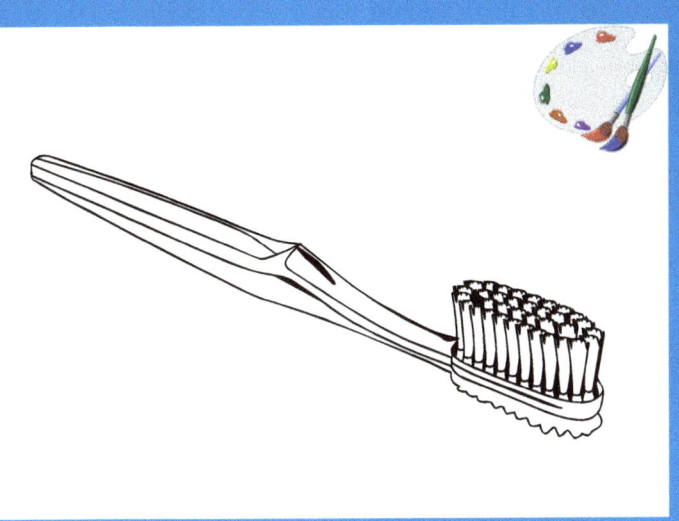

Pronounced as sound of "sh" in "She"

ъ (')
hard sign

Объектив/Ob'yekteev/Object lens

Letter before is hard

Letter before is hard

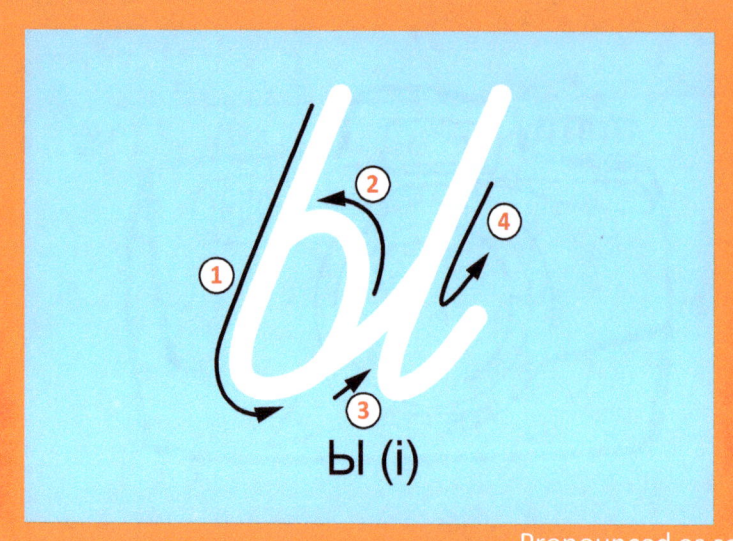

ы (i)

Сыр / Sir / Cheese

Pronounced as sound of "i" in "Ill"

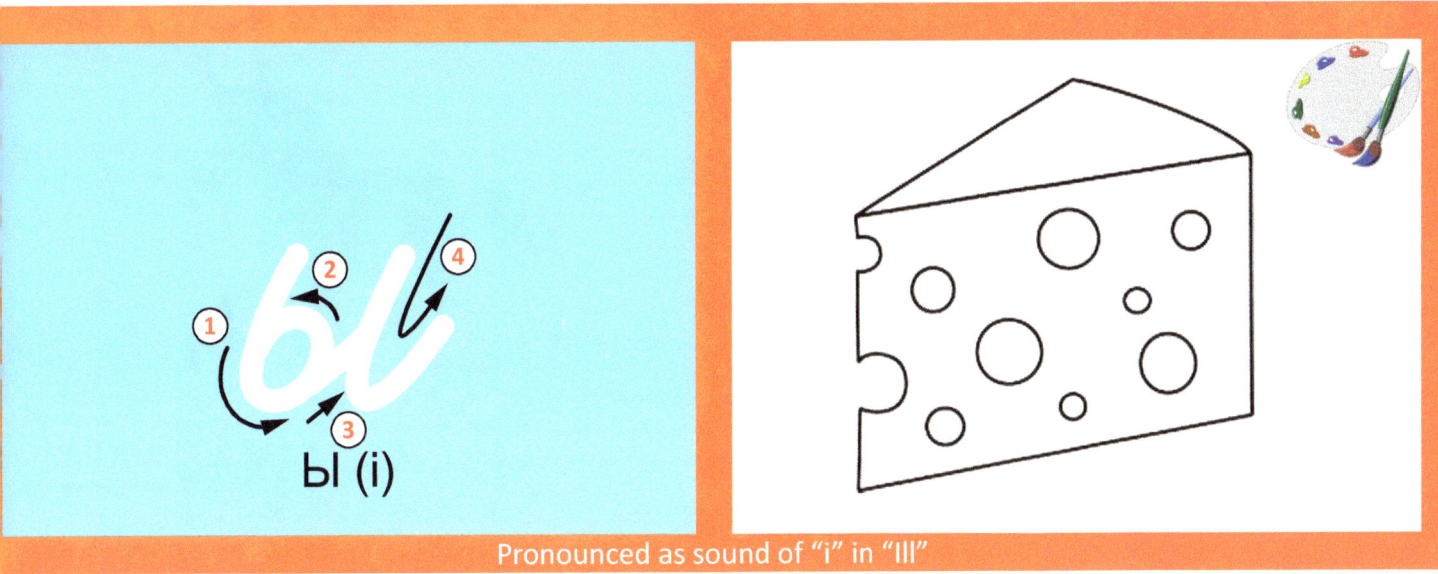

Pronounced as sound of "i" in "Ill"

ь (')
soft sign

Конь/Kon'/Horse

Letter before is soft

Ь (')

Letter before is soft

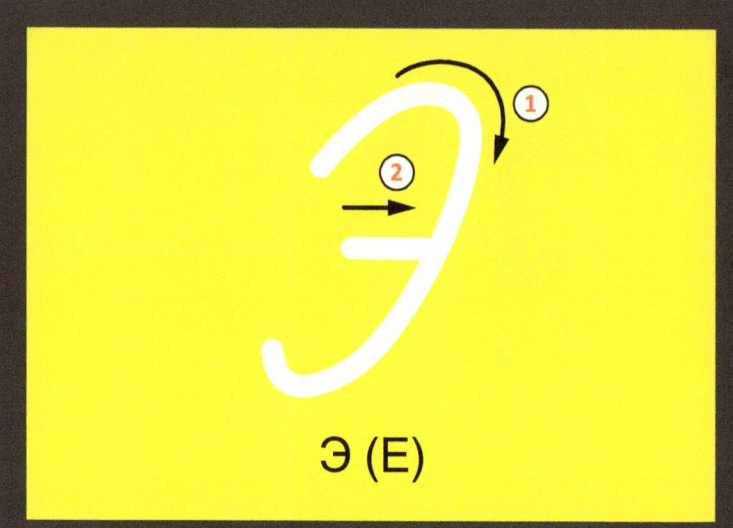

Э (Э)

Экскаватор/Excavator/Excavator

Pronounced as sound of "e" in "Pet"

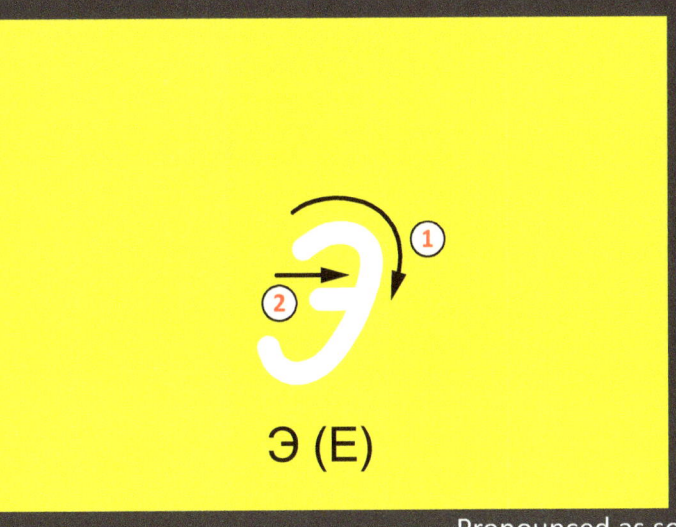

Э (E)

Pronounced as sound of "e" in "Set"

Ю (U)

Юбка / Ubka / Skirt

Pronounced as sound of "u" in "United"

Ю (U)

Pronounced as sound of "u" in "Use"

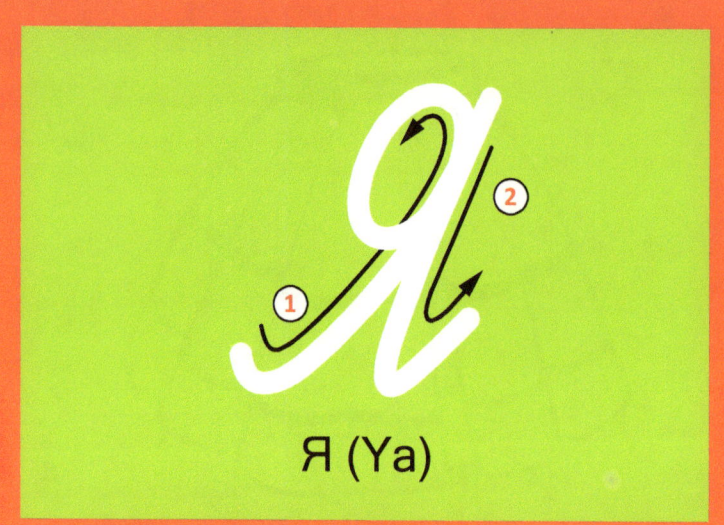

Я (Ya)

Яблоко/Yabloko/Apple

Pronounced as sound of "ya" in "Yard"

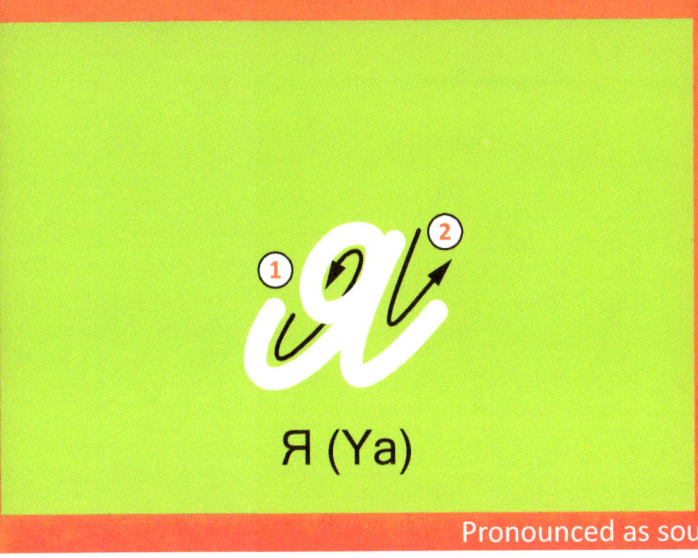

Я (Ya)

Pronounced as sound of "ya" in "Yacht"

www.ingramcontent.com/pod-product-compliance
Lightning Source LLC
Chambersburg PA
CBHW051359110526
44592CB00023B/2891